ABOUT KOJI

The Culture behind the Japanese Food Production. Learn How To Make Shio Koji And Other Koji Recipes. Mold Based Fermentation Process.

MURAOKA HIROMI

© **Copyright 2020 Muraoka Hiromi**

All rights reserved. The content contained within this book may not be reproduced, duplicated or transmitted without direct written permission from the author or the publisher.

Under no circumstances will any blame or legal responsibility be held against the publisher, or author, for any damages, reparation, or monetary loss due to the information contained within this book. Either directly or indirectly.

Disclaimer Notice

Please note the information contained within this document is for educational and entertainment purposes only. All effort has been executed to present accurate, up to date, and reliable, complete information. No warranties of any kind are declared or implied. Readers acknowledge that the author is not engaging in the rendering of legal, financial, medical or professional advice.

Please consult a licensed professional before attempting any techniques outlined in this book.

By reading this document, the reader agrees that under no circumstances is the author responsible for any losses, direct or indirect, which are incurred as a result of the use of information contained within this document, including, but not limited to errors, omissions, or inaccuracies.

Thank you for choosing this book

I wish you a good read and

If you like, leave a short review on Amazon.

Thank You!

Table of Contents

History of Koji 1

Brief chronology of koji 3

Things to know about Koji 28

Falling in Love with Koji 34

Historically Speaking 36

Scientifically Speaking 37

Culinarily Speaking 39

Experimentally Speaking 40

Koji: the Microbe That Makes Miso and Soy Sauce So Delicious 43

What is Koji? 44

The Origins of *Aspergillus oryzae* (aka Koji) 46

Basic Amino Paste Recipe 51

Koji - The culture behind Japanese food production 55

The benefits of Koji 57

Processes 57

Making koji for Clearspring's mirin 58

How To Make Shio Koji 塩麴の作り方 58

How Long Will Shio Koji Keep? 63

Should You Buy Prepared Shio Koji? 63

How to Use Shio Koji 64

Eating Mold 68

How Koji Is Made 69

Using Koji in the Kitchen 69

Health Benefits of Koji 70

Where to Find Koji 71

Koji and the Fermentation Chamber 72

How to Make A Fermentation Chamber 75

How to Grow It 78

What to Do with It 83

Recipes 86

Shio Koji 86

Traditional Vegan Miso 89

Simple Shiitake Dashi 92

Grilled Mackerel with Shio Koji 94

Braised Herb Chicken With Shio Koji 96

Daikon and Cucumber Salad 99

Yakisoba with Shio Koji 101

Simmered Kabocha or Winter Squash with Shio Koji .. 104

Japanese Fried Chicken (Shio Koji Karaage) 106

Homemade Koji Rice 109

CHAPTER 1

History of Koji

Koji is a culture prepared by growing either *Aspergillus oryzae* or *Monascus purpureus* mold on cooked grains and/or soybeans in a warm, humid place.

Koji serves as a source of enzymes that break down (or hydrolyze / digest / split) natural plant constituents into simpler compounds when making miso, soy sauce, sake, amazake, and other fermented foods. Its fragrant white (or red) mycelium, which looks somewhat like the surface of a tennis ball, has a delightful aroma resembling that of mushrooms.

Koji can be divided into two basic types, depending on the type mold used. Most koji is made using *Aspergillus oryzae* (pronounced ass-per-JIL-us oh-RAI-zee). Red rice koji is made using *Monascus purpureus*; it is called beni koji in Japan and hong qu in China; both of these terms mean "red koji." Red rice koji is used primarily as a natural food coloring and as a natural preservative.

Kôji is a Japanese word now widely used in the Western world and non-Chinese speaking countries in the scientific and popular literature on fermented foods, Japanese foods, and natural foods. Koji is written with the exact same character in China and Japan.

In Chinese this character is romanized as qu (pronounced "chew") in pinyin or ch'ü in the Wade-Giles system. Koji was invented in China at least three centuries before the Christian era.

Koji usually serves as the basis for a second fermentation, in which its enzymes help to hydrolyze (break down or digest) basic nutrients. The enzyme amylase (formerly called diastase) digests carbohydrates, the enzyme protease breaks down proteins, and the enzyme lipase (pronounced LAI-pase) digests lipids (fats).

Rice koji, barley koji, and soybean koji are used to make three different types of miso. Koji for Japanese soy sauce is made from a mixture of roasted wheat and defatted soybean meal; this koji is dark-green in color. Whole soybean koji is used to make traditional Chinese soy sauce and fermented back soybeans (also known as Hamanatto, Daitokuji natto, douchi, Chinese black beans, etc.).

Rice koji is used to make both Japanese amazake (pronounced ah-muh-ZAH-kay; non-alcoholic) and sake (rice wine, alcoholic). Koji is to sake as malt is to beer. Each saccharifies the starch (breaks the starch down into sugars) so that these sugars can be fermented to alcohol by yeasts.

Brief chronology of koji

300 BCE – Koji (qu, pronounced "chew") is first mentioned in the Zhouli [Rites of the Zhou dynasty] in China. The invention of koji is a milestone in Chinese food technology, for it provides the conceptual framework for three major fermented soyfoods: soy sauce, jiang / miso, and fermented black soybeans, not to mention grain based wines (incl. Japanese sake) and li (the Chinese forerunner of Japanese amazake).

165 BCE – Fermented black soybeans (made from soybean koji) are found clearly marked in Han Tomb No. 1 at Mawangdui near today's Changsha, Hunan province, in south-central China. The tomb was sealed in about 165 B.C. and was first opened in 1972. The high-ranking lady to whom the tomb belonged was probably the wife of the first Marquis of Tai.

90 BCE – Fermented black soybeans (niequ yanshi qianhe) are mentioned in Chapter 69 of the Shiji [Records of the Historian], by Sima Qian. This is the earliest known history of China and the most famous of all Chinese historical works. Chapter 69 shows that fermented black soybeans (made from soybean koji) (as well as soybeans) had now clearly become major commodities in the Chinese economy.

100 CE – In the Liji (also named Xiaodai Liji) [The Book of Rites], Chapter 6, titled "Monthly Ordinances," contains the earliest known description in Chinese of how grain-based wine (jiu, Japanese sake) was made from millet and rice koji by the Superintendent of Wine.

121 CE – The Shuowen Jiezi [Analytical Dictionary of Characters] contains an early character for qu (koji). It is written with a bamboo radical on top of the word denoting chrysanthemum. The etymology of this character is therefore consistent with the notion that the product was first formed when steamed rice granules were exposed to air in a bamboo basket and that at some time it would acquire the color of the yellow chrysanthemum.

150 CE – The Shiming [Expositor of Names] discusses various types of qu (koji).

544 CE – The Qimin Yaoshu [Important Arts for the People's Welfare], by Jian Sixie contains the first detailed descriptions of how to make qu (koji). Chapters 64-67 deal with both koji and wine. The author gives detailed descriptions of the methods for making nine different types of koji, as well as 37 types of grain-based wines. The nine types of koji are listed in table 20 of Huang 2000 (p. 170). Of these nine, there are actually only four major types. Wheat is the substrate for all except the last one, which uses Setaria millet. Koji is also discussed in this ancient book under jiang, fermented black soybeans (shi), and soy sauce.

725 CE – The Harima no Kuni Fudoki [Geography and Culture of Harima province], from Japan, is the first document that mentions koji outside of China. It states that by the early 8th century in Japan, koji was being made using airborne koji molds.

760 CE – The Manyōshū (Collection of Japan's Earliest Songs and Poems) (from 350-759 CE) mentions koji – the 2nd earliest Japanese work to do so (Yokotsuka 1986, p. 198).

965 CE – The earliest known reference to hong qu (red rice koji; made with Monascus purpureus) appears in China in the Qing Yilu [Anecdotes, Simple and Exotic], by Tao Ku. Among the recipes there is one for red pot-roast lamb, in which meat is simmered with red rice koji) (Huang 2000, p. 193).

1603 – Vocabulario da Lingoa de Iapam [Vocabulary of the Language of Japan], a Japanese-Portuguese dictionary, is compiled and published by Jesuit missionaries in Nagasaki, Japan. There are entries for:

Côji [Koji], a yeast [sic] used in Japan to make sake, or mixed with other things.

Amazaqe [Amazake], a still-bubbling fermented liquid that has not yet completely become sake; or sweet sake.

This is the earliest European-language document seen that mentions koji or amazake.

1712 – In his landmark Latin-language book Amoenitatum exoticarum politico-physico-medicarum [Exotic novelties, political, physical, medical, Vol. 5, p. 834-35], Engelbert Kaempfer is the 2nd Westerner to mention koji (which he calls koos) as part of his description of how miso is made in Japan. Kaempfer lived and traveled in Japan from 23 Sept. 1690 to Nov. 1692 and made many interesting observations. Kaempfer clearly did not understand what koji was, how it functioned, or how it was made. Yet he did realize that "its production requires... the experienced hand of the master."

1766 May – Samuel Bowen starts to export and sell Bowen's Patent Soy, a type of soy sauce that he learned how to make in China and that he started to make at Thunderbolt near Savannah, Colony of Georgia (Georgia Gazette 1766 May 28, p. 1; Hymowitz & Harlan. 1983. "Introduction of the Soybean to North America by Samuel Bowen in 1765." Economic Botany, Dec. p. 371-79).

Bowen must have been the first person to make koji in North America, since he is known to have made good soy sauce and since it is not possible to make good soy sauce without making good koji. He probably made his koji from whole soybeans, but he might have used a combination of wheat and soybeans. Yet how did he get koji starter from China to Savanna? Perhaps he caught natural airborne spores.

1779 – The Encyclopedia Britannica (2nd ed.), under "Dolichos," mentions koji (which it calls koos, after

Kaempfer) in English – as part of its description of how miso is made in Japan.

1783 – Koji (called Koos, after Kaempfer 1712) is mentioned for the 3rd time in English by Charles Bryant in his Flora Diaetetica. It is included in a description of how to make miso.

1797 – The Nihon Sankai Meisan Zue [Illustrations of Japanese Products of Land and Sea] contains the earliest known illustration of koji being made in Japan; the koji is then shown being made into sake.

1818 – Basil Hall, in his Account of a Voyage of Discovery to... the Great Loo-Choo Island [Okinawa or Ryukyu] states: "... hard boiled eggs, cut into slices, the outside of the white being colored red." The red color was probably imparted to the outside of the shelled eggs by red rice koji.

1867 – Koji is mentioned in English in A Japanese and English Dictionary, by James C. Hepburn. It states: "Koji: Malt made by fermenting rice or barley, in the process of making sake, and soy [sauce]." This was also the first time that koji was incorrectly called "malt." Also: "Koji-buta: A shallow box for holding malt."

1870-1889 – The modern field of microbiology (actually bacteriology) is pioneered in Europe by Ferdinand Cohn, Robert Koch, and Louis Pasteur. The identification and classification of microorganisms begins.

1874 – Prof. J.J. Hoffman of Leyden, Netherlands, then a professor in the medical school of Tokyo University, publishes a 4-page paper in German titled Ueber die Bereitung von Schoju, Sake und Mirin (On the Preparation of Shoyu, Sake, and Mirin) in the Mittheilungen der Deutschen Gesellschaft fuer Natur- und Volkerkunde Ostasiens (Yokohama). Not long before this (but at an unknown date) he had published a translation of an article on sake from the Japanese Encyclopedia (1714) (Atkinson 1881, p. iii) – making these the first two documents in European languages that discussed koji in detail. However no names of microorganisms appear in this article.

1876 – The Official Catalogue of the Japanese Section: And Descriptive Notes on the Industry and Agriculture of Japan, by the Imperial Japanese Commission to the International Exhibition at Philadelphia contains a good description of how to make soy sauce using koji made of wheat and soybeans. It begins (p. 112): "The soy, or 'soyu,' is made of a small bean, the 'Dolichos hispida,' to which are mixed wheat, salt and water. The beans are first boiled, and the wheat bruised and steamed; both are then mixed with a small addition of fermenting wheat [koji], placed in flat wooden boxes and kept for several days at fixed temperature in a special room. At the end of three days, the mass [koji] is all covered with fungi and partly with roots of germination..."

1878 March 10 – "Kōji no Setsu" [Theory of Koji] by H. Ahlburg and Shinnosuke Matsubara published in Japanese in Tokyo Iji Shinshi (Tokyo Medical Journal), p. 12-16. This article contains the terms Eurotium, and E. Oryzae Ahlbg. The koji mold was originally named Eurotium oryzae Ahlburg; in 1884 it was renamed Aspergillus oryzae

(Ahlburg) Cohn by Cohn. Western knowledge of microbiology is rapidly reaching Japanese scientists.

1878 Sept. 12 – R.W. [Robert William] Atkinson, a British professor (D.Sc.) at the University of Tokio [Tokyo], writes a 3-page article titled "Brewing in Japan,"published in the prestigious scientific journal Nature (London). Interested in the new science of microbiology, he is one of the first three Westerners to study and understand koji in depth, he is the first who writes in English. In describing a visit to sake breweries situated in Hachioji near Tokio, he gives a detailed description of how koji is made from tané (spores), then how sake is made from koji. This is the earliest English-language document seen that mentions tané, the mold spores from which koji is made, or that mentions the use of wood-ash in making koji or that mentions "the friend of tane" [tomo koji].

1878 Dec. – Mr. O. Korschelt, in Japan, publishes a 19-page paper titled Ueber Sake (On Sake) in the Mittheilungen der Deutschen Gesellschaft fuer Natur- und Volkerkunde

Ostasiens (Yokohama). It contains a detailed discussion of koji and how to make it.

1880 April – A paper by R.W. Atkinson (in Japan) titled "Preliminary Note on the Action of the New Diastase, Eurontin, on Starch" is read to the Chemical Society, London. This is the earliest English-language document seen that contains the word "diastase" used to refer to the starch-splitting enzyme today called "amylase."

1881 March – R.W. Atkinson expands his 3-page article into an 81-page monograph titled "The chemistry of saké-brewing," published in Memoirs of the Tokyo Imperial University Science Department. His discussion of koji and its preparation, of its active properties and its action upon cane sugar and maltose, is much more detailed and knowledgeable than before. This is the earliest English-language document seen that describes how to make koji on a commercial scale. He notes that in Tokio, koji is made in long tunnels cut into the clay, 25-30 feet long and 15-20 feet below ground level. He uses the word "ferment" to refer to what would soon (by May 1881) be called an enzyme.

1881 May 1 – R.W. Atkinson writes "On the diastase of koji." Diastase would soon be called an enzyme. Atkinson states: "I feel that some apology is needed for using the Japanese word kôji, but as there is no foreign product in any way resembling it, I have thought that there would be less danger of confusion arising by retaining the Japanese word than by using the word 'malt.' As will be seen from the following description, the nature of this substance is quite different from that of malt, so that the use of that word might lead to erroneous impressions."

1891 Feb. 20 – The first article about Jokichi Takamine's work with koji appears in the Chicago Daily Tribune. Titled "Whiskey to be cheaper. Discovery of a new and better process of manufacture. From 12 to 15 per cent can be saved over the old method – Takamine a Japanese, the inventor – He sells his secret to the trust – It will be immediately utilized. Prospect of a reduction of the retail price." it explains that he wants to replace malt with koji in the process of making whiskey in Peoria, Illinois. This is also the earliest publication seen that mentions Jokichi Takamine or that mentions the words "koji" or "moyashi" in connection with him. He is now a resident of Chicago, the husband of an American woman (née Caroline Hitch), an expert chemist, and head of the "Takamine Fermenting Co." [probably Takamine Ferment Co.]. He has made tests of his new process at the Phoenix and other distilleries in Peoria.

1891 Feb. 28 – First article about the work of Jokichi Takamine that mentions diastase (a starch-digesting enzyme now, called amylase) is published in the Peoria Herald (Illinois, p. 8).

1891 March 7 – A major front-page article, by the Associated Press, appears in the Los Angeles Times. Titled "'Microbe straight.' The new drink that barkeepers will serve," it begins: "Chicago, March 6. The Takamine Ferment Company, organized by the Whiskey Trust to exploit a new process of whisky-making invented by the Japanese chemist Takamine, has increased its capital stock to $10,000,000." This is the earliest document seen that mentions the "Whiskey Trust" in connection with Mr. Takamine.

1891 June 17 – Jokichi Takamine, a Japanese chemist residing in Chicago, applies for his first U.S. koji patent. However he has already secured patents in Canada, Belgium, France, and Austria-Hungary.

1891 Sept. 24 – Another major article about Jokichi Takamine appears in the Chicago Daily Tribune (p. 7). Peoria – "For several months the Distillers and Cattle Feeders' company [whisky trust] has been experimenting with the Takamine process of making whiskey." Takamine "has been here personally conducting the experiment. The distillers are so well pleased that they have decided to fit up the Manhattan distillery with new machinery. The new plan greatly reduces the cost of manufacture. A queer feature is that a species of bugs found on the rice is used instead of yeast for the fermenting process." No: A species of mold is used instead of malt.

1891 Oct. 8 – A fire of unknown origin, which started shortly after midnight, burned one building at the Manhattan Distillery (3 story brick building at South Water St., Peoria), which "was being fitted for experiments in the manufacture of Tackimine [sic, Takamine] whiskey." (Peoria Transcript, p. 8, col. 3).

Peoria fire department records show that there was no major fire in 1893 – as was later often reported in literature about Takamine.

1891 Oct. 12 – Takamine applies for his first British koji patent, No. 17,374. A fungus of the genus Aspergillus is grown on steamed rice to make Taka-Moyashi and pure Taka-Moyashi. "Tané-Koji (or seed koji) or Moyashi, is a term that as been heretofore applied to a yellowish green mouldy mass, consisting of steamed rice covered by a Mycelial fungus, bearing yellowish green spherical cells, and has the property of producing both diastase and ferment cells. It has not heretofore been designated by any specific name and, and I call it 'Aspergillus Koji.'" This is the earliest document seen in which the word

"Aspergillus" or the terms "Tané-Koji" or "ashes of trees" are used in connection with koji or with Dr. Takamine.

1892 April 17 – Yet another major article about Jokichi Takamine appears in the Chicago Daily Tribune (p. 6). He has apparently survived the fire and now, for the first time, we learn that his koji is made from "wheat bran" which is much less expensive than other substrates for producing koji enzymes.

1894 Feb. 23 – Jokichi Takamine applies for his earliest patent (U.S. Patent No. 525,823) which contains the word "enzyme" (or enzymes") or the terms "diastatic enzyme" or "taka-koji" or "tane-koji" in connection with koji. This was the first patent on a microbial enzyme in the United States. This enzyme "possesses the power of transforming starch into sugar."

"Takamine, in 1894, was probably the first to realize the technical possibilities of enzymes from molds and to introduce such enzymes to industry" (Underkofler 1954, p. 98).

1894 Nov. 27 – The last article about Jokichi Takamine's work with koji and whiskey in Illinois appears in the Peoria Transcript (p. 2). Titled "Distilleries to start: There will be a resumption of business at once," it states that at the Manhattan distillery "the Takamine process will be tested with further improvements made during the season. The distilling business is now looking up."

1894 – Takamine moves his Takamine Ferment Co. to Chicago make diastase on a relatively small scale based on his 1894 patent.

1895 July – Parke, Davis & Co. of Detroit, Michigan is now making and aggressively marketing Taka-Diastase. After its efficacy became more widely known, Jokichi Takamine contracted with Parke, Davis for full-scale manufacturing and marketing of the product (Parke, Davis 1895 July; Kawakami 1928, p. 36).

This is the earliest known commercial enzyme made in North America. Dr. Clifford W. Hesseltine states (1991): "Dr. Jokichi Takamine was the father of commercial enzymology."

Takamine recognized that the diastatic properties of the Aspergillus enzyme had potential medical applications. Parke, Davis & Company marketed Taka-Diastase as a digestive aid for the treatment of dyspepsia said to be due to the incomplete digestion of starch. Taka-Diastase was enormously successful and Takamine became a consultant to the company.

1897 Dec. – With Parke, Davis as his patron, Takamine moves his family to New York from Chicago and establishes an independent laboratory on East 103rd Street in Manhattan [New York]. He soon founded the International Takamine Ferment Company and the Takamine Laboratory.

1897 – Yamamori Jozo-sho (Yamamori Brewery), at 561 North 6th Street, San Jose, California, is the earliest known company to make shoyu (Japanese-style soy sauce) in the United States. To make shoyu, they must have made koji. So they were the 2nd company in North America to make koji for use in making soy sauce.

1898 Jan. 21 – Jokichi Takamine, at the New York Section of the Society, presents a long, brilliant paper titled "Diastatic substances from fungus growths" which is published in the Journal of the Society of Chemical Industry (London) on Feb. 28 (p. 118-20). This is the earliest document seen in which Takamine mentions "taka-diastase," the digestive enzyme he has patented.

1899 – Jokichi Takamine receives the degree of Doctor of Chemical Engineering from the Imperial University of Japan, and in 1906 the degree of Doctor of Pharmacy (W.W. Scott 1922, p. 371). Hereafter he is widely referred to as "Dr. Takamine."

1906 – The Karuhorunia Miso Seizo-jo [California Miso Manufacturing Co.] at 262 Brannan St., San Francisco, California, is the earliest known company to make miso in the United States. In a 1906 ad (in Japanese) they describe themselves as manufacturers of Japan miso. To make miso, they must have made koji. So they were the first company in North America to make koji for use in making miso.

Other early Japanese makers of miso and koji in the United States were: Yamane Miso in Sacramento, California (1907) and Kodama Miso Seizo-sho in Los Angeles (1908).

1908 – Kodama Miso Seizo-sho, at 310 Crocker St. in Los Angeles, California, is the earliest known company to make and sell koji in the United States. They advertise their koji as Shiro Koji ("White Koji").

As noted above, they also use this koji to make their own commercial miso.

1909 June 16 – "A preliminary note on the varieties of Aspergillus oryzae," by Teizo Takahashi is published in the Journal of the College of Agriculture, Tokyo Imperial University. He isolated three varieties of molds from three kinds of koji starter (tane koji) from three sources (sake, miso, and shoyu).

1913 – Marusan Joto Shiromiso, at 607-609 North Alameda, Los Angeles, is the 2nd earliest known company to make and sell koji in the United States. They advertise their koji (in English) as "Special Koji." Hence they are the first to advertise koji in English in the USA.

1915 Nov. – The Takamine Laboratory, which makes and does research on Taka-Diastase and other koji products, moves to Passaic, New Jersey – about 10 miles west of Manhattan. Joe Takamine, Jr. is now in charge of this facility (Scott 1922, History of Passaic and Its Environs, Vol. III, p. 372).

1952 summer – "The Distillers' and Cattle Feeders Trust," by Earnest E. East is published in the Journal of the Illinois State Historical Society (p. 101-23). The best scholarly summary seen of Dr. Takamine's work and troubles in Peoria.

1970 July 7 – The catalog of The Erewhon Trading Co., Inc. titled Traditional Foods states: "Koji rice, imported from Japan, will be available soon." Why would young Caucasian Americans want koji? So they can make their own miso and amazake. Erewhon is a pioneer in the macrobiotic, the natural-foods, and the soyfoods movements; these three movements soon give rise to a rebirth of interest in koji.

1971 Oct. – An article in East West Journal (p. 6; the flagship national macrobiotic publication) titled "Making Miso" mentions that "Erewhon will introduce to the domestic market a yeast grain called koji, essential to the production of miso."

1971 – Cornellia Aihara, in "Macrobiotic child care" published in Macroguide (Chico, California) No. 8 (41 p.) describes how to make amasake at home using "2 cups sweet brown rice. ¼ cup koji, and 4 cups water." Note: Koji is now being made in Chico by Junsei Yamazaki, who uses it to make "Yinnies," an organic grain-based chewy candy or sweet syrup, for Chico-San Inc.

1973 Sept. – An article in The Macrobiotic (Chico, California, No. 92, p. 22), titled "Miso making with white rice koji," states: "Koji is rice or wheat, barley, etc. which has been treated with a mold called succaromises [sic, Saccharomyces is a yeast genus]. Koji rice (only white rice unfortunately) is available in Japanese food stores."

1976 Sept. – The Book of Miso, by Shurtleff and Aoyagi (Autumn Press), contains a chapter titled "Koji cookery" (p.

162-63, with detailed recipes for amazaké, daikon pickled in koji, and eggplants pickled in koji) followed by extensive, illustrated information about making koji and koji starter at home (the earliest such document; p. 177-82). Koji is also mentioned on a total of 97 pages throughout the book.

1977 Aug. – Miso Production, by Shurtleff and Aoyagi (Soyfoods Center), describes (with many illustrations) how to make koji and miso on a commercial scale – for people who want to start and run a business. The first book of its type.

1978 May – Miyako Oriental Foods, Inc., a miso manufacturer in Los Angeles, California, launches Cold Mountain Firm Granular Rice Koji, which it makes. A leaflet explaining how to use koji accompanies the product. The package design, product name, and product concept were developed by William Shurtleff and Akiko Aoyagi at the request of Mr. Noritoshi Kanai.

1979 March 13 – The first Caucasian-run miso company in North America, the Ohio Miso Co., in Monroeville, Ohio, founded by Thom Leonard and Richard Kluding, begin making miso and koji on this date. Thom has been making miso on a small, noncommercial scale since 1974. Other Caucasian-run North American miso companies that (of course) also made their own koji were:

1979 April - Shin-Mei-Do Miso (by Lulu Yoshihara; Denman Island, BC, Canada).

1981 Oct. American Miso, Inc. (by John Belleme; Rutherfordton, North Carolina).

1982 Oct. South River Miso Co. (having bought out Ohio Miso Co. in Nov. 1980, Christian and Gaella Elwell started their own production in Oct. 1982 in Conway, Massachusetts).

1993 Sept. – Bibliography of Koji, by Shurtleff and Aoyagi published (Soyfoods Center; 535 references, 151 pages).

2000 Dec. – Vol. 6, Biology and Biological Technology. Part V: Fermentations and Food Science, by H.T. Huang is published in the Science and Civilisation in China series, by Joseph Needham. This book contains vast amounts of information about the early history of qu (koji) in China.

2002 Jan. – "Takamine Jokichi and the transmission of ancient Chinese enzyme technology to the West," by H.T. Huang is published as a book chapter in Chan et al. Huang observes: "When we talk of technology transfer in the last hundred years, we tend to think of the traffic as flowing entirely from West to East."

2004 – Professor Emeritus Eiji Ichishima of Tohoku University, Japan, proposes that the koji mold, Aspergillus oryzae, be called a "national fungus" (kokkin), much like national or state birds, flowers, trees, or animals – in the prestigious Nippon Jozo Kyokai Zasshi (Journal of the Brewing Society, Japan); his proposal is approved at the society's annual meeting in 2006.

2012 April – The Art of Fermentation, by Ellix Sandor Katz is published by Chelsea-Green Publishing Co (xxiii + 498 p.). Katz describes himself as a "fermentation revivalist."

CHAPTER 2

Things to know about Koji

Can supply enzymes that modern people lack

Enzymes are a type of protein that helps digest food, synthesize new cells, and burn fats and sugars. It also works to eliminate active oxygen that causes illness and aging. It is the power of these enzymes that keeps us healthy.

Enzymes are found in fresh vegetables, fruits and fish, but they are sensitive to heat and lose their effectiveness when heated. Processed and cooked instant foods do not contain enzymes at all.

That's where Jiuqu comes in.

Jiuqu contains a variety of enzymes produced during the fermentation process.

I want to take in the enzyme of Jiuqu well and keep it forever.

It becomes delicious just by pickling

When meat and fish are pickled in salted rice, the proteins and starches of the ingredients are decomposed into amino acids, glucose and maltose. Amino acids are umami ingredients, and glucose and maltose are sweet ingredients, so people feel that they have become delicious.

In addition, the enzymes contained in the Jiuqu break down the ingredients, making the meat and fish tender and easier to digest and absorb.

Just pickle the fish the night before, put it in the fridge and bake it quickly in the morning, and the cheap salmon will be amazingly delicious. You might be told, "What happened to you suddenly becoming a good cook?"

Amazing sweetness without sugar

Yamazaki Amazake does not use any sugar or additives. The natural sweetness of Jiuqu is surprisingly sweet. This sweetness is created by the decomposition of rice starch into glucose by the enzymes of Jiuqu.

Most of the amazake on the market contains sugar and additives, so people who drank " Jiuqu-only amazake " are surprised that "It's so sweet but it doesn't contain sugar? Really !?" Yeah.

Amazake is a highly nutritious drink similar to an intravenous drip.

In the process of fermenting rice by Jiuqu, vitamins such as vitamins B1, B2, B6, pantothenic acid, inositol, and biotin are produced in amazake. In addition, rice protein is broken down into amino acids by Jiuqu. Amazake is one of the ingredients that contains the most essential amino acids.

It is said that the high nutritional components of amazake have much in common with the nutritional supplements provided by intravenous drip in hospitals.

Indeed, " drinking drip ".

During the Edo period, people drank chilled amazake as a measure against heat fatigue.

In addition, it was recommended to give it to postpartum women who are worried about breast milk production.

People in the old days knew it.

Until the Jiuqu is made:

- Wash the rice

Yamazaki Koshiibuki uses Koshiibuki from Niigata.

Even if it is cooked as it is, it is made only with delicious new rice, so the grain is large and the shape is uniform.

- Steam the rice

Transfer the sharpened rice to a large steamer and steam it. If it is steamed too much, it will become too soft and sticky, so adjust the steaming time so that the grains become fluffy.

- Sprinkle the steamed rice with Jiuqu.

When it is steamed, put it in a transport machine and carry it to the room.

Since the heat of the rice can be removed while it is being carried by the machine, sprinkle it with Jiuqu at the outlet of the transporter.

- Let it lie in the room

A room is like a sauna with a temperature of 30 degrees and a humidity of around 95%. Jiuqu sprinkled on rice propagates in a hot and humid room and produces enzymes.

- Loosen, cool, and smooth the rice

When the rice is left in the room for a while and the Jiuqu bacteria proliferate actively, the temperature of the rice rises. In addition, Jiuqu grows hyphae and the rice hardens. When the temperature rises, the Jiuqu will burn (the Jiuqu will heat up and darken the color), so in order to maintain the proper temperature, you should loosen the rice, make a heap of rice, or even out it.

- Get out of the room

On the third day, fluffy Jiuqu can be seen from the rice. Take it out of the room and let it cool overnight. Even if the fungus is not noticeable on the outside, the hyphae firmly bite into the center of the rice and it becomes white when cracked.

- Jiuqu completed

Packed in a bag, " Yamazaki Jiuqu shop's raw yellow Jiuqu " is completed.

The Koji is sweet sake Shiokoji , soy sauce koji will be to the original, such as.

Two kanji, "糀" and "jiuqu". Which one?

It is to "malt", "koji" and the Chinese characters of "Koji There is a native script (Japanese-made Chinese characters) that".

"Jiuqu" uses wheat as a raw material.

"Jiuqu" is a national character created by looking at the mold that grows like a flower on rice, so it refers to rice that is used as the raw material.

In general, all koji are sometimes referred to as "jiuqu", but since Yamazaki Kojiya uses rice koji, it is referred to as "jiuqu".

Falling in Love with Koji

I'm in love with a mold. I know this seems a bit odd, pretty weird even, but my work as a zymologist is driven by my fascination with the transformative actions of bacteria, yeasts, and molds on foods. Falling in love with a microbe isn't all that strange in my world. When a relationship like this one blossoms, monumental advancements take place within gastronomy.

These microbes are the ones responsible for some of our most beloved foods. Cheese, chocolate, beer, bread, pickles, and miso are all foods that we love dearly, so why shouldn't that feeling be parlayed to the beings responsible for making them?

I fell in love with the mold known as koji a little more than two years ago, while working with my friend Jonathon Sawyer at Tren-tina. Chef Sawyer asked that I start making miso out of garban-zo beans for use as an ingredient. Koji, whose scientific name is Aspergillus oryzae, is the mold responsible for the autolysis, or breakdown, of beans into a fermentable medium. You simply cannot make miso without koji. This was the start of a love affair that has grown into an undying passion for me.

When you work with fresh koji, it's easy to understand how one can fall under its spell. Molds responsible for making foods like blue cheese and charcuterie smell either sour or of ammonia, or they reek like a damp cellar or wet dog. Koji smells like a sweet fra-grant combination of apples, fresh yeast, champagne, and honey-suckle.

When you smell it for the first time, you see why people decided to use it as a food more than 9,000 years ago. It's irre-sistible. Foods made with koji contain such depth of complex and nuanced tastes and flavors that they are unrivaled.

After 9,000 years of dominance in Asia, koji is finally embarking on a much-welcomed global conquest, making an appearance in restaurant kitchens from Copenhagen to St. Petersburg, Mexico City, and even Cleveland. You don't have relegate koji to Asian-style foods. It's just as much at home with a burger and fries as it is with miso soup and sushi. I predict that in the next five to seven years, koji, in some shape or form, will be a go-to ingredient in your kitchen.

Historically Speaking

Koji has a long and varied history. It's believed that it was domes-ticated shortly after rice, somewhere around 7,000 BCE on the Korean Peninsula or in China. After domestication, its users real-ized it could transform the unfermentable long-chain starches in rice into simple fermentable sugars. Its discoverers also realized it could do the same for the complex proteins found in beans by turning them into extremely tasty amino acids.

After these discoveries, people developed many applications for koji, and it spurred countless types of foods. The most commonly known ones are Japanese: soy sauce, miso paste, and sake. Ver-sions of these foods exist in their own unique ways in China, the Koreas, Thailand, Vietnam, Taiwan, and several other Asian and Southeastern Asian countries. In fact, within each country there are several diff erent versions of each of these foods. Koji is Japan's national mold. Koji makers in Japan are so revered, that they enjoy the same status we grant to our celebrity chefs. Koji's magic is that powerful.

Scientifically Speaking

Koji is a mold, and molds are fungi. Fungi are enchanting organ-isms that are so distinct in their physiology and morphology, they have a taxonomic kingdom all to themselves.

The lifecycle of a mold or fungus begins as a spore. The spore is something akin to the seed of a plant or the egg and sperm of an animal. Once a spore starts its life, it produces tiny filaments called hyphae. These hyphae eventually form mycelium, a dense mass that resembles the roots of a plant. The hyphae and myce-lium grow on and in various substrates, wood, insects, soil, and animals, and break them down using enzymes. The fungus then absorbs the remaining base nutrients after this breakdown.

Koji produces two types of powerful enzymes—protease and amylase—as it grows on cooked grains or seeds or just about any-thing. Proteases break down proteins, and amylases break down carbohydrates. Koji is unique because of how fast it does this.

Once koji spores have been incubated on cooked rice or other foods, the fl avor, taste, and aroma changes associated with this enzymatic breakdown are fully noticeable within 48 hours. That's incredibly fast. It may take many months to see a similar transfor-mation if you were to look at this process in a fruiting fungi, such as oyster mushrooms.

Culinarily Speaking

Soy sauce, miso paste, and sake are just the tip of the iceberg. Many more foods are made using koji. Two of the most prominent are Amazake (sweet koji) or Shio (salted koji). These two foods are made by mixing koji with cooked rice and water in Amazake, and koji with water and salt to yield Shio. Both Amazake and Shio are used to make a variety of foods or even consumed as is.

The Japanese drink Amazake is consumed for its healthful proper-ties, much as many Americans drink kombucha or other hip pro-biotic beverages. Amazake is also an important ingredient in sake and rice vinegars. When pitched with yeast, Amazake ferments into sake, which can then be fermented into vinegar.

Shio is used as a seasoning when cooking and also as a medium to cure or pickle vegetables and proteins. Other uses include making a variety of amino (umami) sauces, ice cream, and baking bread.

Experimentally Speaking

Years ago, I had an epiphany. Given koji's traditional uses and its ability to transform foods, could I harness this in a new and surprising way? Could I use koji as an age-accelerant for fresh cuts of meat and seafood or for charcuterie? I decided to put this to the test.

The first thing I did was set out on a mission of academic research. I couldn't find any easily accessible information about using koji in this way. So I reached out to various people in Japan to see if this was some-thing that had been done before. Again, nothing. After that I decided to just go for it.

My first test was growing the mold on scallops. I figured that if I could do that without spoiling them, I was on to something. I gently seasoned the scallops, coated them with rice fl our and koji spores, then set them up in an incubation chamber with 95% humidity at 90° for 48 hours to culture. When I checked them after the 48-hour time limit, I was amazed. The intoxicatingly delightful aroma of koji mixed with the crisp briny aroma of the scallops was so intense that I started to salivate. I cooked them up immediately and was further amazed. The flavor, taste, and texture were unlike any food I had ever experienced.

This spurred more investigation and experiments. Beef, llama, venison, lamb, duck, chicken, and a host of grains, seeds, and pulses were all sub-jected to koji culturing. Each experiment yielded a food that amazed and enchanted my colleagues and me.

I also realized how fast this process is. I could create a koji-cultured steak in two days that was comparable to a 30-day dry-aged steak. Cuts of charcuterie that would normally take two months or more to make using traditional methods were ready to slice and eat within 14 days. This was truly unique, not only due to this accelerated timeline but also due to the intoxicating aroma, flavors, and tastes developed by the koji.

Koji's uses and results in the kitchen are so magical that once you ex-perience them, you'll become as passionate as I am. From an aging and charcuterie accelerant, to a seasoning and pickling medium, the uses for koji are just beginning to be explored in a broader and nontraditional context. I'm curious to see where this wonderful modern embrace of an ancient food might lead us.

CHAPTER 3

Koji: the Microbe That Makes Miso and Soy Sauce So Delicious

For those big into fermentation and who are looking to add a new living organism into their rotation, may we recommend reading up about koji? Koji, the microbe that brings those intense umami flavors to Japanese cuisine, can be harnessed to not only ferment liquors and soy sauce, but to quickly and efficiently age charcuterie and cheeses.

Ahead you'll find an introduction to what, exactly, koji is, for a foundational understanding of this beloved organism. When you've proven educated on the subject, you can move on to attempting some of your own koji alchemy, like fermenting amino paste (aka miso), which only requires three key ingredients—koji being the main one. These amino pastes can be added into a number of things—from chicken noodle soup to tomato sauce, hummus, and even chocolate ice cream—amplifying flavors with that extra umami hit.

Like other fermentation projects, you'll need to map out a few weeks, and up to a few months, to allow the fermentation to properly click into place, but the final result is well worth the wait.

What is Koji?

Koji is an amazingly transformative and seemingly magical ingredient that has bewitched many people over thousands of years. One of the many things koji does is turn complex carbohydrates into simple sugars via powerful enzymes it produces in order to feed itself. It is a type of mold used in the production of many foods such as miso, soy sauce, sake, jiang, douchi, amazake, makgeolli, meju, and tapai just to name some. Koji has been used for millennia throughout Asia and most recently, in the past 150 years or so, has been slowly conquering the rest of the world in ways that the people who first domesticated it could hardly conceive. Take the charcuterie that Jeremy makes at Larder Delicatessen & Bakery. After the meat is cured and inoculated with koji, the drying time is cut by as much as 60 percent. Imagine being able to make a prosciutto in six months instead of two years.

Koji is an extremely powerful organic technology that has not only shaped the foods of various peoples but also ingrained and transformed their very cultures. Actually, virtually every culture that encounters koji or a food made with or from it becomes entranced by its transformative power. The Japanese have declared it their National Mold and have even created comic books in which it is featured as a cartoon character! We feel that in order to truly understand what it is and what it's capable of, we must know a little about how, where, when, and why it came to be. When investigating these matters, it's always best to start at the beginning in order to give a complete understanding. That beginning would be koji's evolution.

The Origins of *Aspergillus oryzae* (aka Koji)

The koji mold, Aspergillus oryzae (or, as we will refer to it going forward, simply koji), has a bit of mystique surrounding its origins. Due to rigorous scientific research, we know that koji evolved when it was domesticated from the highly toxic A. flavus. Dr. John Gibbons at Clark University in Worcester, Massachusetts, is currently leading the way in research related to how koji evolved away from its toxic ancestor, by identifying the traits and genetic changes that accompanied the domestication of A. oryzae.

To address this topic he and his team sequence and compare the genomes of A. oryzae and its toxic progenitor species, A. flavus. They then use computational genomics, evolutionary biology, and population genetics to pinpoint genetic differences between domesticated and wild genomes. When the genetic differences are present in genes whose functions are known, they design laboratory experiments to test how these genetic differences change the characteristics of A. oryzae.

They're essentially attempting to use biology to understand the traits that ancient artisans selected for when they domesticated A. oryzae. These findings have evolutionary, cultural, historical, and applied significance, which makes this system so exciting to many of us.

Why would an individual decide to conduct research on something so specific as koji? Well, when Dr. Gibbons went to college, he wasn't fully aware of filamentous molds and their uses. He had always been a big-picture person and applied to graduate school knowing that he wanted to study genomics, indifferent as to what his specific organism would be. After interviewing with labs that studied fruit flies, humans, yeast, plants, and molds, Gibbons ended up joining Dr. Antonis Rokas's lab at Vander- bilt University, where one of the major research areas was Aspergillus (the koji genus) genomics. Gibbons was given a stack of papers to read when he started at the Rokas Lab so that he could see which areas would be of most interest for him to research. One paper he read completely blew him away. He had assumed that only plants and animals had been domesticated by humans, but a number of papers called A. oryzae "domesticated."

One particular paper detailed how the publishing group used a combination of chemistry and archaeology to determine the contents of a nine-thousand- year-old pottery jar from China. They were able to show that the pottery held a fermented drink composed of rice, honey, and fruit, and that this type of fermentation required a mold that was really good at breaking down starches into sugar. It confirmed that humans have been making rice-based alcohol for nine thousand years through the help of filamentous fungi! The biology and genomics, cultural aspects, and applied side of this topic were exciting for Gibbons.

With the promise of potential research ahead, Gibbons dove in on a quest to unlock the how, why, when, and where of koji's domestication. For more than ten thousand years, humans have been taming plants and animals for particular characteristics. For example, domesticated plants usually produce more fruits or seeds than their wild progenitors thanks to selective breeding. Domestication has a profound impact on the genome of any given organism, and koji is no exception. Specific mutations underlie many of the traits selected for in domestication. For example, a single change in the genetic code of maize (corn) from its progenitor teosinte led to "naked grains" as opposed to the nearly impenetrable kernels of teosinte that are encased with silica and lignin. These mutations were shaped by selective breeding over long periods of time; when you simply compare the phenotype (essentially the way something looks) of teosinte with that of maize, you can easily observe these changes. And while plants and animals primarily shape our collective knowledge of the genomic and phenotypic effects of domestication, a number of bacteria, yeasts, and molds were also domesticated.

I've read some of Dr. Gibbons's papers about koji and its pathway to domestication, and they are nothing short of fascinating! To under- stand koji's impact on various cuisines and cultures, we felt it important to establish an understandable timeline for its evolution and domestication. Dr. Gibbons points out that we define domestication as "the genetic modification of a species by breeding it in isolation from its ancestral population in an effort to enhance its utility to humans."

As I've noted, the domestication of koji occurred at least nine thousand years ago. Noncoincidentally, according to Dr. Gibbons, this is roughly the same time rice was domesticated (the two often go hand in hand). It makes sense that as rice was domesticated, the mold that eats it, koji, would follow suit in its new agricultural home. He also points out that people have been selling koji dating back to the thirteenth through the fifteenth centuries in China, a considerable amount of time before Western science even knew what microbes were.

To put this into relative perspective, it would still be roughly three hundred years before Robert Hooke would first observe dead plant cells under a microscope, followed by others observing living organisms.

The exact answers to the questions surrounding koji's evolution and domestication are yet to be found, and the process is quite puzzling due to the fact that koji and its toxic ancestor, Aspergillus flavus, share 99.5 percent of their genome. But the important point is that koji has been used in food production in China since at least 7000 bce, making it one of the oldest domesticated foods on the planet.

Basic Amino Paste Recipe

When it comes to applications, amino pastes have way more potential than has traditionally been explored. We've put them into chicken noodle soup, burgers, tomato sauce, pierogi, hummus, cookies, pies, jam, and chocolate ice cream, to name just some of the successes.

An all-time favorite of ours is a compound butter made with amino paste, which we use for everything from sautéing vegetables to schmearing on a bialy. The beauty is that the paste is so concentrated and has so little moisture that you don't need to adjust a recipe in most cases. There are reasons that miso has become ubiquitous around the world: It's versatile, relatively inexpensive, and scrumptious. The key is to think of amino pastes as salt with a greater depth of flavor.

This is the master recipe that we use for nearly all our amino pastes, whether we make them from soybeans to beef heart. We've kept it simple and straightforward so that you can easily memorize it. It can be scaled up or down as you desire by either multiplying or dividing the ingredients. You can make 20 pounds (9 kg) just as easily as you can make 2 pounds (900 g). Try to take into account how much of the paste you plan on using and adjust the measurements appropriately. For both light and dark basic amino paste, fresh koji is preferred, but if you're using dry koji, mix in 25 g (about 1 fluid ounce) of lukewarm water into the koji in a small bowl and allow it to hydrate for a couple of hours at room temperature. If you don't want to wait, process into a rough paste.

Note: For ferments applications, we recommend using grams to measure rather than their US equivalent. This assures an accurate salt percentage for food safety.

Basic Amino Paste

Ingredients

- Light (2 weeks–3 months): 250 g koji
- 25 g kosher salt
- 250 g protein
- Dark (6 months–1 year+): 165 g koji
- 65 g kosher salt
- 330 g protein

Instructions

1. Add the koji and salt to a medium mixing bowl. With clean hands, mix the koji and salt together so the latter is evenly distributed. Now combine mixing and squeezing the koji and salt together to break down the koji into a paste as much as possible. Don't worry too much about making it super fine or missing some grains; the pieces will have the opportunity to break down fully during the fermentation process.

2. If the protein is in a solid form and cannot be simply mixed into a paste, process accordingly. Most ingredients can be cut up into chunks and run through a food processor.

3. Add the protein base and mix thoroughly. Pour the contents into any non-reactive pint container. A mason jar is preferred. Store the jar at ambient temperature for the specified time for either light or dark miso.

CHAPTER 4

Koji - The culture behind Japanese food production

Koji is the culture behind Japanese food production, discover what it is and how it is used.

Koji is not actually a yeast, as many people mistakenly believe. Koji is cooked rice and/or soya beans that have been inoculated with a fermentation culture, Aspergillus oryzae. This naturally occurring culture is particularly prevalent in Japan, where it is known as koji-kin, which explains why so many Japanese foods have been developed over the centuries using it. It is used to make popular foods like soya sauce, miso, mirin and sake.

The first step in making these products is creating the koji. This involves adding the Aspergillus culture to steamed rice or soya beans or, in the case of shoyu soya sauce, to a combination of steamed soya beans and roasted, cracked wheat. The resulting mixture is then placed in a warm and humid place for up to 50 hours, often in wooden trays called koji buta in Japanese. During this time the Aspergillus feeds on the rice or soya beans, using enzymes that are adept at breaking down carbohydrates and proteins.

Once it has been created, the koji is usually added to larger quantities of rice or soya beans, together with a brine solution. In the case of mirin, it is mixed with glutinous rice and the distilled alcoholic beverage shochu. In each case, the enzymes in the koji break down complex carbohydrates and proteins into amino acids, fatty acids and simple sugars.

When making sake, rice is mixed with koji, which breaks down the carbohydrates into sugars then subsequently fermented by yeast to produce alcohol and carbon dioxide.

The benefits of Koji

The amino acids, fatty acids and simple sugars released by the action of the koji add flavour, depth and, it has been argued, a number of health benefits to foods. For example, the fermentation of soya beans using koji to create miso is known to increase the levels of isoflavones, which are compounds that are said to be effective in the prevention of cancer.

One of the amino acids released by the action of koji is glutamate, which imparts an intensely satisfying and delicious savoury taste known as umami. This, combined with the simple sugars also released, ensure that foods made using koji have a uniquely rounded and deep flavour.

Processes

Fluffy white grains of rice koji, here being used to make sake.

Making koji for Clearspring's mirin

Clumps of rice are broken up to ensure that the koji develops in a uniform way.

The rice inoculated with kojikin culture is placed in wooden trays in a warm, humid atmosphere to propagate.

Miso is just one of the many traditional Japanese foods that relies on koji...

...as is sake, here served in a traditional wooden container called a masu.

How To Make Shio Koji 塩麹の作り方

Japanese Ingredient Highlight: Shio koji (塩麹, 塩糀). A century-old natural seasoning used in Japanese cooking to marinate, tenderize, and enhance umami flavor of a dish. Learn more about this all-purpose seasoning.

It's been several years since Shio Koji (塩麹, 塩糀) experienced a huge resurgence in popularity as a versatile seasoning in Japan. This section is about shio koji, its benefits in cooking, and how to make it at home.

What is Shio Koji?

Shio koji (塩麹, 塩糀) is a natural seasoning used to marinate, tenderize, and enhance the umami, or richness (one of the five basic tastes) in foods. It's made of just a few simple ingredients: salt, water, and rice koji.

Rice koji (米こうじ, 米糀, 米麹) is steamed rice that has been treated with koji mold spores (Aspergillus oryzae, koji-kin 麹菌, or koji starter). Koji is a specific strain of mold that has been cultured over the centuries.

You may feel hesitant to eat it and wonder why we make rice moldy on purpose. But you have most likely eaten it already!

Koji has been the key ingredient to make miso, soy sauce, sake, mirin, rice vinegar, amazake, shochu, and shio koji. It's a live food that is rich in enzymes that break down starches and proteins in food into sugars and amino acids.

You can use shio koji to marinate meats, make pickles, flavor your vegetables or use it as a salt substitute. In a recipe that calls for one teaspoon of salt, you can substitute with 2 teaspoons of shio-koji. Shio-koji is really versatile and can be used in any kind of cooking.

Benefits of Shio Koji

Because it is a fermented ingredient, shio koji is known for its many health benefits, which includes:

A natural pro-biotic seasoning

- Tenderizes food
- Brings out the umami and sweetness in foods
- Reduces the intake of salt
- Aids for digestion
- Clear the skin
- Anti-aging
- Contains minerals, fiber, and vitamins

How to Make Shio Koji

To make shio koji, you will need some form of grain koji. As mentioned earlier, grain koji is made by inoculating some form of cooked grain (most commonly rice) with koji kin and then drying it. If moldy long-term science projects are your bag, you can pick up a copy of The Noma Guide to Fermentation to learn how to make grain koji for yourself. Or you can purchase ready-to-use, granular rice koji—dried, koji kin-inoculated rice—online or in Japanese markets and even in some high-end supermarkets (look for it in the same refrigerated section where you'd find miso).

Once you have some rice koji on your hands, the process for turning it into shio koji couldn't be simpler, but it does take at least a week to ferment. Combine rice koji with kosher salt in a lidded container and then stir in water until the salt has dissolved. The general ratio for shio koji is 5:4:1 by weight of water to grain koji to salt (the ratio is adjusted slightly in the attached recipe to accommodate volumetric measurements).

Once the mixture is well-combined and the salt is dissolved, pop the lid on your container of shio koji in the making and find an out-of-the-way spot in your home to ferment it at room temperature. The only hands-on work you have to do during the fermentation process is to stir the mixture once per day. This ensures that the rice grains are being evenly coated with the liquid, which will take on an increasingly milky color as well as a sweet and funky aroma.

After a week, the shio koji will thicken to a porridge-like consistency and will smell fruity and pleasantly fermented. Depending on the time of year and the temperature in your home, this fermentation process might take a day or two longer, but it will be good to go between seven and ten days. At this point, pop the shio koji in the fridge and store it there until you'r ready to use it.

How Long Will Shio Koji Keep?

Like miso and soy sauce, shio koji will keep for a long time in the fridge in an airtight container.

For this reason, I like making big batches of shio koji that I can dip into whenever I want to give a protein the shio-koji marinade treatment or add some funky sweetness to a sauce or dressing.

Most recipes for shio koji claim that it can be refrigerated for up to six months, but the 10-month-old batch I had was still perfectly good and showed no signs of degradation in quality. It's hard to imagine a batch of shio koji going bad before you use it up (provided you store it properly).

Should You Buy Prepared Shio Koji?

Prepared shio koji is available for purchase, but I don't recommend using it. When I was experimenting with shio koji, I tested a lot of store-bought shio koji and found that most commercial versions were overly sweet and often had alcohol added to prolong their shelf-life. The added sugars in these versions of prepared shio koji change their flavor and make them harder to cook with, causing foods to brown and burn much too quickly. While making it yourself requires some advance planning, it's worth it and doesn't require any significant effort.

How to Use Shio Koji

So you've made a batch of shio koji, and it's now sitting in the back of your fridge waiting for you to unleash its potential. So how should you go about using it? First and foremost, it's one of the easiest and most effective marinades around. But shio koji has other uses as well! Add it to sauces, dressings, baked goods, lacto-fermented vegetables, and more! Here are some of my favorite uses for shio koji, which I will continue to add to as I experiment more and more with it in the test kitchen.

Marinade for Poultry, Meat, and Fish

The most common use for shio koji is as a marinade or cure for poultry, meat, seafood, and even vegetables. For proteins, slather them up with shio koji and let them hang out for as little as 30 minutes and up to 24 hours, depending on the size and type of ingredient you are working with.

Generally speaking, the larger the piece of food, the longer you should marinate it. Over time, shio koji will begin to cure the ingredient it's in contact with, so delicate foods, like fish, should be marinated for a shorter amount of time.

You can decide whether to leave the texture of the shio koji as-is, in its porridge-like state, or buzz it up with a blender to make a smooth, creamy marinade. It will be effective either way. I usually blend it when I am looking to get a smooth, burnished surface on the end product (I have a recipe for koji roast duck dropping soon), and leave it coarse when marinating something that will have a crust-like exterior (such as a beef roast).

When you're ready to cook, wipe off excess shio koji from the surface of your food to prevent it from scorching and then cook as you normally would, although you do have to keep an eye on things since koji-treated ingredients do take on color much faster (as is the case with most marinades that usually contain some form of sugar).

Individual fish fillets, scallops, and shrimp can be marinated for as little as 30 minutes with shio koji, which will firm them up, keep them succulent, and season them with a perfect balance of savory and sweet flavor.

Steaks, chops, chicken breasts, and the like should be marinated for at least an hour and up to a few hours.

Larger cuts, especially bone-in pieces of meat or poultry, are best marinated overnight (at least 12 hours), giving the protease enzymes time to do their magic, breaking down proteins and seasoning the meat. Treat large roasts as if you are dry-brining them: set them on a wire rack-lined baking sheet after slathering them with shio koji. As with regular kosher salt, the salinity in shio koji will work its way into the meat and dry out the surface of the roast at the same time.

For smaller items that you aren't searing or roasting (like the koji duck confit recipe that I will be publishing soon), you can marinate them in sealed zipper-lock bags.

Flavor Booster for Sauces

Shio koji can also be used to bump up the flavor of sauces and dressings. Add savory depth to a gravy or jus by stirring in a little blended shio koji. Try it in salad dressings—koji Caesar salad is killer, I promise you—or whisked into your favorite pan sauce. Shio koji has a can't-quite-put-your-finger-on-it magic flavor that toes the line between savory and sweet in the best way, and there is so much room for exploration with it. So go make yourself a batch, and start koji-cooking!

CHAPTER 5

Eating Mold

Koji is a culture made up of a certain fungus (mold) called Aspergillus oryzae, which has been used to ferment rice and soybeans in Japanese, Chinese, and Korean kitchens for centuries. Koji can actually have other involved fungi, but Aspergillus oryzae is the most common, and therefore the names can be used interchangeably. Its end purpose is to enhance the flavor of items like soy sauce, sake, and miso.

Fungus-infused rice may seem unappetizing, but this mold is one of the good guys and is a far cry from the fuzzy mold you see on expired food or fruit that has overstayed its welcome. It has been so valuable in Japanese culinary traditions that it has been honored with the title of "national fungus" by Dr. Eiji Ichishima of Tohoku University.

How Koji Is Made

The initial step in creating koji is to add the fungus to a steamed food that needs to be fermented. After the two ingredients are combined, they are typically left to up to 50 hours in wooden trays, called koji buta. This cozy, humid environment allows the fungus to work its magic by using enzymes to break down proteins into amino and fatty acids, and complex carbohydrates into simple sugars.

Using Koji in the Kitchen

After its initial fermentation, koji is often added to larger batches of rice or soybeans, along with a brine solution to create a rich umami flavor for a particular food or drink.

One of the biggest uses of koji is in sake (a popular Japanese rice wine). To make sake, steamed rice is combined with koji, and after complex carbohydrates are broken down into simple sugars, yeast is added to ferment the sugars that enable it to become this popular spirit. Mirin, a sweet rice wine, is also made in a similar fashion.

Koji rice can also be made into a seasoning called shio koji that can add a burst of flavor to meat, be used as a base for flavoring pickles, or simply as a healthier salt substitute.

Soybeans are also commonly used with koji to produce the rich, complex flavors that are present in soy sauce and miso. The process for creating these iconic Japanese condiments is very similar to producing koji rice. By mixing cooked soybeans and the koji culture together for miso, or roasted, crushed wheat and the koji culture for soy sauce, you arrive at these well-loved, umami-laden condiments.

Health Benefits of Koji

The health benefits of koji are numerous, including having probiotic properties that include aiding in digestion to boosting your immune system. There have also been studies that have demonstrated that koji-rich foods like miso and soy sauce contain isoflavones that can help prevent cancer.

Where to Find Koji

Koji starters are not something you would find commonly next to the milk in your grocery store or even in a local Asian specialty market. Since they are live cultures, your best bet is to get these cherished microbes online.

If you prefer to leave the scientific experimentation to the professionals, you can get your dose of shio koji in Japanese supermarkets in sauces, salad dressing, and seasonings.

CHAPTER 6

Koji and the Fermentation Chamber

Once again, Koji is an extremely useful edible mould that has the potential to help solve a lot of global problems like, hunger, malnutrition and effective organic farming.

In this section, I will show you how to grow your own koji at home or in a professional kitchen. If you're savvy you could even turn your new fermentation and koji growing knowledge into something useful that will make you money.

Aspergillus oryzae. The biological name for the species of mould responsible for giving us koji. It's a filamentous fungus that can be grown on many substrates like rice, barley, vegetables and anything else rich in carbohydrates.

It's been used in Asian countries for centuries in the making of soy sauce, miso, douchi, and alcoholic drinks like amazake (low alcohol), sake (medium alcohol), and Shōchū (high alcohol).

Koji's usefulness lies in the fact that it produces a huge range of enzymes when grown on a substrate. Up to 50 different enzymes have been found.

The most useful to us being amylases which break up carbohydrates into it's building blocks, sugars, and proteases that break up proteins into it's building blocks, amino acids.

Examples of how these work are, miso and sake.

In miso, the soybeans have a high protein content and when mixed with koji, salt, and water the soybeans disintegrate because the amylases cleave the carbohydrates and the proteases the proteins.

A once bland and indigestible ingredient gets turned into one of the most delicious umami-rich, nutrient-dense foods known to mankind.

When making miso, a mould strain producing high protease is selected, and grown at a specific temperature, to promote high protease development instead of amylase.

With sake, the opposite is done. A high-amylase producing strain of mould is selected and the mould grown within a specific temperature range to promote amylase production.

The amylase then cleaves the carbohydrates in a carbohydrate-rich ingredient, like rice, into simple sugars, which the yeast in sake brewing can consume and turn into alcohol.

The mould produces these enzymes in order to free up the building blocks it needs to survive and eventually sporulate.

Most of the time we stop the process at the time enzyme production is at it's highest. Other times you might choose to let the mould spore in order to harvest more spores for next time you want to grow koji.

In order to grow, it needs a specific environment. And, as we have seen, different temperatures yield different results depending on what we want to make with it.

Let's look at what you'll need to do this at home.

How to Make A Fermentation Chamber

You need a little incubation set up to properly make koji. You could wing it but chances are you will probably mess it up and give up altogether, which is not the desired result.

Don't worry, all you need is the following:

- An insulated box - Could be a small wooden cabinet, Styrofoam box or even an unused fridge or freezer.
- Thermostat and humidity controller
- Heating mat

- Small humidifier
- Clean linen cloth - Any will do.
- Tray to grow the koji in - Either flat or perforated to allow for airflow.

The point to all this is to create an environment where the temperature and humidity can be kept constant.

To set this up plug your two controllers into a power socket and then connect your heating mat to the thermostat and the humidifier to the humidity controller.

This is all very easily done. I barely passed math at school so I'm sure you will manage it too.

Jumping ahead but, sometimes we ferment or age an ingredient at 60C. Your heating mat won't reach that temperature. I insulated my fridge doors with aluminium foil and use a small fan heater to reach and keep that temperature.

It doesn't consume too much electricity once the temperature is reached and very little energy to maintain the temperature when well insulated.

For home use, you could use a rice cooker or slow cooker to ferment at higher temperatures. It's what I use when doing small batches.

Simply set your thermostat to 59C and then plug the rice cooker or slow cooker set to keep warm into the thermostat. More on that another day.

Ingredients Needed

You need mould spores to grow koji. I list a few places I've bought from before at the end of this section.

Soaked barley and koji tane

- 1000g Pearl barley
- 4g Koji tane (I always use more than suggested on the packet in case the potency of the spores have gone down a bit)

You either need the pure Aspergillus Oryzae spores or Koji tane. A white powder which is spores mixed with rice flour or blended dried rice koji that has fully spored.

If you buy pure spores you need to mix it with lightly toasted white flour that's been cooled down.

We toast the flour to sterilise it and mix the spores in flour to ensure even distribution when inoculating a substrate.

How to Grow It

The process is very simple. However, you will need practice to get it perfect. Like anything in life.

1. Steam the barley for about 45 minutes or until fully cooked. Do not boil it as it would ruin the process and drown the mould.
2. Sterilise all your utensils and hands. Also, boil or steam the linen cloth. This is to make sure no bad bacteria gets involved.
3. Once your barley is cooked, cool it down in a separate sterilized tray or bowl to about 35C. Sprinkle over the Koji tane and mix well. This is to inoculate the barley with spores.
4. Line your perforated or flat tray with a slightly damp cloth (not wet) and spread the inoculated barley out and cover with the cloth completely.

5. Place into your incubation setup. Place the thermostat needle into the barley and let the humidity controller sensor dangle close by.

Now the real fun starts.

Depending on the purpose, we need the Koji to produce either more protease or more amylase. This means that we need to maintain a temperature of 28C(82F) - 30C(86F) for protease production and 30C(82F) - 34C(93F) for amylase production.

For that reason:

1. Set your thermostat to maintain a temperature of either 28C(82F) or 32C(89,6F). Set your humidistat to 70% and makes sure the humidifier is switched on and has enough water.
2. Place a buffer like a bowl or wire rack in between the warming mat and the tray with barley so that there is some circulation and the barley does not directly touch the heating source.

3. Close the incubation chamber and keep an eye on the temperature. You can connect the thermostat and humidistat to your phone via Wi-Fi so that it tells you when things are changing.
4. We now start a 48-hour cycle. Over the next 12 hours, the koji will start "infiltrating" the barley. At some point, it will start to form a mycelium and the koji will produce its own heat. When this happens we have to break it up and cool it down.
5. We want the temperature to stay within range. So, break it up and spread it out when the temperature jumps. Don't worry if the temperature goes a bit above the maximum limit. Just don't let it stay there for too long.
6. Keep this up until 48 hours are finished and the barley is covered in a thick mycelium of white mould.

You now have fresh koji. Taste it. It's delicious just like that.

If you made koji to produce protease, it should have a mushroomy flavour, a bit like the rind of camembert cheese. If you made it to produce amylase, it will have a sweeter aroma and flavour, a bit similar to very ripe apricots.

Once you have tasted koji you can not un-taste it. You will immediately be able to identify it in naturally brewed soy sauce, miso, and sake.

To store for later use simply store airtight in the freezer. Otherwise, you can dry it out for longer storage or store in the fridge for up to a week.

Fluffy white mycelium of koji mould on barley

You don't have to grow koji on barley or rice. It can be grown on many substrates. For instance, when making soy sauce you grow it directly on soybeans and toasted cracked wheat, or a combination of others. Here's a list of just some of the substrates you can also use.

- Bread - One of the more creative ways to use up old bread. The Noma fermentation book has a wonderful rye miso recipe you could follow. In my kitchen, I use Borodinsky bread or sourdough leftovers from the previous day. Any other bread will work.

- Sweet potato - Vegetables are also a great substrate to grow it on. The book, Koji alchemy, concentrates on that a lot.
- Peeled beans - Make sure the beans are fully cooked but not mushy and peel the outside skin off. Otherwise, the mould will not be able to break through the tough skin and start growing.
- Buckwheat - Tricky but doable. Good for those that love a challenge.
- Split peas - Instead of using barley or rice to grow it on for miso, try growing straight onto split peas (green or yellow) and then mix with more cooked split peas, water and salt to make stunning miso.
- Lentils - Lentil shoyu (soy sauce), is one of the things I made that always surprises my clients most when doing tastings for them. I use a mixture of different lentils blended with toasted crushed wheat and grow aspergillus sojae on it. It then goes into a salt brine and ferments for months.

- Quinoa - Also one for the brave but, miso and soy sauce made from quinoa is absolutely outstanding.

What to Do with It

Once you have grown it, the possibilities of what to do with it are almost endless. Below are a few traditional and non-traditional products to make with it.

- Soy sauce - Once you've made your own, you won't ever use store-bought soy sauce again.
- Miso - One of the easiest most versatile koji ferments to make.
- Sake - Made by using rice koji and extremely tricky but, very rewarding when done.
- Shio koji - A cure or marinade made with salt, koji and water. Used to briefly marinate beef, chicken or fish.
- Flour - Dried and ground up into a fine powder. Used in bread making and baking.
- Amazake - Lightly fermented low alcoholic drink.
- Koji milk - Dried koji blended with water and strained.

Fuzzy barley

Where to Buy Spores

Here are a few companies I've used in the past to buy it. They are all slightly different but they are all very helpful and good at what they do.

- Fermentation Culture - They also produce their own shoyu, miso and other ferments. (non-affiliate)
- Good old Amazon - This strain is best for making soy sauce. (affiliate)
- Organic cultures - They stock tons of others mould and interesting spores too. Also, has great information and how-to section. (non-affiliate)
- Bio'c (product site) - This is the best quality I've bought. It's a longer wait than the others though, and the dealing with the post etc is a bit of a pain. But, worth the effort. (non-affiliate)

Useful Equipment for This Recipe

- Mini fridge
- Digital temperature controller thermostat

- Digital humidistat controller
- Humidifier
- Heating mat

CHAPTER 7

Recipes

Shio Koji

Prep Time: 20 mins | Cook Time: 0 mins

Japanese Ingredient Highlight: Shio koji (塩麹, 塩糀). A century-old natural seasoning used in Japanese cooking to marinate, tenderize, and enhance umami flavor of a dish. Learn more about this all-purpose seasoning.

Servings: 2 (jars)

Ingredients

- 200 g rice koji (7.05 oz)
- 4 Tbsp sea salt (50 g; salt can be 10-30% of koji quantity - Do not use table salt)
- 1 cup water

Instructions

1. Gather all the ingredients.
2. In a large bowl, break and separate the koji grains into smaller pieces.
3. Rub the koji firmly in hands to separate into individual grains.
4. Rub the koji until aromatic, add salt and mix all together.
5. Add water. If necessary, add more water if it doesn't cover the surface of koji. Rub the koji with your hands.
6. Transfer to sterilized jar(s)/container with a lid. Make sure the shio koji are submerged in water, if not, add more water.
7. Ferment the shio koji at room temperature, open the lid and mix it once a day for 1 week during summers and 2 weeks during winters (as warmth temperature speeds up the ripening process). Add a bit of water if the shio koji is too hard. It might taste salty at the beginning, but it will gradually become mild. Shio Koji will become thicker and

begin to smell sweet from the fermentation. Store in the refrigerator for up to 6 months.

Traditional Vegan Miso

There are two miso recipes that use ingredients other than fish, which make them perfectly suitable for vegans. If you order shiitake and kombu dashi miso at your favorite Japanese restaurant, there is no need to worry. That's because mushrooms and seaweed replace the fish in these miso varieties.

In addition, some contemporary recipes allow you to create a tasty vegan miso in your own kitchen. Thus, there is no need to scratch your head and ask "is miso soup vegan?" Just roll up your sleeves and follow one of these recipes to get the best homemade vegan miso soup.

Miso Noodle Soup

This vegan miso recipe gives you a perfect combination of vegan flavors and a reinvigorating punch we have come to like in miso. Follow the instructions below, and you'll have two tasty servings of miso in about half an hour.

Ingredients

- 2 tbsp of miso paste
- 1 tbsp of grated fresh ginger
- 1 tbsp of sesame seeds
- 1 minced garlic clove
- 1 spring onion
- 2/3 cup of Soba noodles
- 1 1/3 cup of chestnut mushrooms
- 4/5 cup of tofu
- 1 broccoli head
- 1-liter of vegetable stock
- A handful of green beans and snap peas

Instructions

1. Slice the spring onion and leave the greens for later. Then put the slices in a big pot and fry them on sesame oil until they soften. Once the slices are soft, add the minced garlic and the ginger and cook for another minute.
2. Now, you can add the miso paste together with a ladle of vegetable stock. Stir the mix until the miso

is completely liquefied. When the miso liquefies, add the rest of the stock and simmer the mix.

3. While simmering, add the chopped mushrooms and cook for another five minutes. Then add the broccoli and the beans and cook for five more minutes. At the same time, you can prepare the soba noodles following the instructions on the bag. The noodles go at the bottom of the serving bowl.

4. In the end, add the tofu cubes to the miso soup along with the snap pea pods and cook for a couple more minutes.

5. Once everything blends nicely together, pour the soup over the soba noodles and garnish it with the spring onion greens and sesame seeds.

Miso soup tastes the best if eaten straight from the pot. You should thus let it cool ever so slightly, and eat the miso as soon as it's cool enough to sip.

Simple Shiitake Dashi

As previously mentioned, shiitake dashi is a miso soup variety that is suitable for any vegan palate. It is also very easy and quick to prepare. There are only three ingredients in this recipe, so there is no reason you shouldn't give it a try.

Ingredients

- One 6-inch kombu piece
- 4 dried shiitake
- 7 cups of water

Preparation

1. First, you need to soak the shiitake and kombu in water for about 15 minutes. There is no need to use a separate dish—you can soak them in the pot you use for cooking. After 15 minutes, take the shiitake out, remove their stems, and then slice the mushroom heads.
2. Now, you can put back the sliced mushroom heads and bring the pot to a simmer at medium heat. A five-minute simmer is enough for the kombu to

release all of its flavors, so after the simmer, you can remove it from the soup.
3. Leave the shiitake on for another 15 minutes until they are properly cooked. At this point, you can add other vegetables to your shiitake dashi and continue cooking until everything is nice and tender. To add some extra flavor, you can use a tablespoon of soy sauce or mirin (Japanese rice wine).

Shiitake dashi also works really well with udon or soba noodles, though the noodles might require some extra seasoning. There is one extra tip for shiitake dashi: if you want to get the most of the dried shiitake mushrooms, you should leave them to soak overnight.

Grilled Mackerel with Shio Koji

Low in calorie and rich in protein, this dish makes a lean and healthy option for everyday cooking. Marinating the mackerel with Shio Koji allows the flavor to permeate throughout the flesh. Also grilling the fish lends it a crispy light char and leaves the inner fillet meat 'melt-in-your-mouth' tender.

Prep Time 10 minutes | Cook Time 15 minutes

Total Time 25 minutes | Servings 2

Ingredients

- 2 small fillets (⅓ lb, 150g) mackerel
- 2 tbsp Hikari Miso Shio Koji
- Lemon wedges

Instructions

1. In a flat container, put mackerel and Hikari Miso Shio Koji together and marinate for at least 30 minutes.
2. Grill or broil the fish at 350F (180C) for 25-30 minutes. Or pan fry the fish over medium low heat.

3. Serve immediately with slices of lemon

Recipe Notes

Quick Tip: Adjust the marinating time according to the size of your mackerel fillets.

Braised Herb Chicken With Shio Koji

Shio koji accentuates the flavor of chicken simmered to perfection. With rosemary and oregano in a white wine broth, this braised chicken will tantalize the palate.

Prep Time 10 minutes | Cook Time 40 minutes

Total Time 50 minutes | Servings 2

Ingredients

- 4 (1 lb) bone-in, skin-on chicken thighs (rinsed and pat dry)
- 2 tbsp. Hikari Miso Shio Koji
- 2 cloves garlic (minced/crushed)
- 1 tbsp. all-purpose flour
- 1 tsp. paprika
- ½ tsp. dried rosemary (or 1 tbsp. fresh rosemary)
- ½ tsp. dried oregano (or 1 tbsp. fresh oregano)
- 1 tbsp. olive oil
- 1 thin carrot cut into 2 inch thick slices
- ½ large onion cut into 4 wedges
- 1 cup chicken broth

- ¼ cup dry white wine
- 1 lb small red potatoes

Instructions

1. Put the chicken, shio koji, and garlic in a large plastic bag and massage ingredients together. Marinate in the bag for 30 minutes.
2. Add flour, paprika and herbs to the bag and shake to coat.
3. Heat oil in a Dutch oven over medium heat. Place chicken (skin side down) and remaining marinade into the Dutch over.
4. Cook 3 minutes on each side or until lightly brown.
5. Add carrot and onion and cook for 2-3 minutes, stirring constantly.
6. Add broth, wine, and potatoes and bring to a boil.
7. Reduce heat and simmer covered for 40 minutes or until chicken is done and vegetables are tender.

Recipe Notes

Quick Tip: You can marinate the chicken for up to 2-3 hours. You can also experiment with different herbs!

Daikon and Cucumber Salad

This is a simple yet surprisingly flavorful daikon radish and cucumber salad recipe created by Nami of JustOneCookbook.com. Shio Koji's malt ferments the vegetables resulting in a lightly pickled mix that can be served as an appetizer or side salad.

Prep Time 5 minutes | Servings 2

Ingredients

- 1/2 lb. daikon radish (peeled)
- 2 Japanese cucumbers or ½ of an English cucumber
- 1/4 cup carrots (julienned)
- 2 tbsp. Hikari Miso Shio Koji
- 1/2 tbsp. rice vinegar
- 1 tsp. sesame oil
- 1 red chili (chopped, if you prefer less spicy remove the seed)

Instructions

1. Cut daikon and cucumber diagonally while rotating them a quarter between cuts. This Japanese cutting technique is called "Rangiri."
2. Put daikon, cucumber, carrot, and all the seasonings in a large closable plastic bag.
3. Remove the air from the bag and massage the vegetables and make sure they are blended well with the seasonings. Keep the bag in the refrigerator for 45-60 minutes for best flavor.
4. Serve this dish cold or at room temperature. Store in the refrigerator for up to 24 hours.

Recipe Notes

Quick Tip: The Japanese cutting technique "Rangiri" will provide more surface area for vegetables to absorb flavors.

Yakisoba with Shio Koji

Yakisoba is a perfect quick meal everyone loves. Shio koji colors the flavor of this Japanese stir-fried noodle dish with savory and salty notes. Garnish with benishoga (red pickled ginger) and sprinkle on some aonori (dried green seaweed) to finish.

Prep Time 10 minutes | Cook Time 15 minutes

Ingredients

- 1/2 lb 8 oz, 225 g sliced pork belly, cut into 1 inch pieces
- 1 tbsp Hikari Miso Shio Koji (for marinating pork belly)
- 2 tbsp vegetable/canola oil
- 2 cloves garlic (sliced)
- 2 cups 5.5 oz, 156 g chopped cabbage (about 4 cabbage leaves)
- 1 1/2 cup 3 oz, 85 g bean sprouts
- 1/3 cup 1 oz, 25 g julienned carrot
- 3 servings/packs yakisoba noodles (375 g)

- 1 tbsp sake (you can substitute with 1 tbsp water for sake)
- 2 tbsp water
- 2 tsp soy sauce
- 2 tbsp Hikari Miso Shio Koji
- Aonori (dried green seaweed to sprinkle on top)

Instructions

1. Put the pork belly in a bowl, add Hikari Miso Shio Koji and marinate for 30 minutes.
2. Heat a wok or pan with oil over medium high heat. When the oil begins to smoke, add the garlic and meat and stir-fry until the meat is no longer pink.
3. Add the cabbage, bean sprouts, and carrots into the wok and stir-fry until they are tender.
4. Add the noodles, sake, water, soy sauce, and Hikari Miso Shio Koji. Continue to stir until the noodles are well blended with the seasonings and completely cooked through. Transfer to plates and sprinkle aonori. Serve immediately.

Recipe Notes

Quick Tip: Try making yakisoba with different ingredients such as shrimp, chicken, and sausages! When you season yakisoba noodles, add one tablespoon of Shio Koji at a time and taste before you add more.

Simmered Kabocha or Winter Squash with Shio Koji

Soft simmered kabocha squash or Japanese pumpkin is a favorite of every age group. Cooking the kabocha with Shio Koji instead of the usual soy sauce makes it more flavorful and adds another layer to its sweetness.

Prep Time 5 minutes | Cook Time 5 minutes

Total Time 10 minutes | Servings 4

Ingredients

- 12 oz. kabocha/winter squash
- 1 tbsp. Hikari Miso Shio Koji
- Water

Instructions

1. Cut the kabocha into 1-inch cubes and put into a medium saucepan
2. Add just enough water to completely cover kabocha, and add Hikari Miso Shio Koji

3. Bring to a boil then lower the heat to simmer. Cook the kabocha until a skewer goes through smoothly, about 4-5 minutes
4. Cover with a lid and set aside to allow the flavor to slowly be absorbed. You can serve this dish cold

Recipe Notes

Quick Tip: Do not overcook kabocha squash initially; it will get mushy and lose its shape and appeal. Allow it to slowly cook with the residual heat while it absorbs flavor from the shio koji.

Japanese Fried Chicken (Shio Koji Karaage)

Karaage or Japanese-style fried chicken can be more exciting with Shio Koji marinade. Juicy and packed with flavor, this dish will keep you coming back for more.

Prep Time 10 minutes | Cook Time 15 minutes

Total Time 25 minutes | Servings 4

Ingredients

- 1 lb (450g) boneless chicken thigh with skin cut into 1 inch pieces
- 4 tbsp. Hikari Miso Shio Koji
- 1 tsp. grated ginger
- 1 tsp. crushed grated garlic
- 1 tsp. soy sauce
- ½ cup potato starch or corn starch
- Vegetable/canola oil for deep frying
- Lemon wedges to serve

Instructions

1. Combine the chicken with Hikari Miso Shio Koji, ginger, garlic and soy sauce in a bowl or large plastic bag and marinate for at least 30 minutes (or up to 1 day).
2. Heat up a pot of cooking oil for deep-frying. Ideal temperature is about 320-335F (160-170C).
3. When the oil is almost ready, add the potato starch in the bowl or plastic bag with the chicken. Mix and coat the chicken with the starch.
4. Gently drop each piece of chicken into the pot and deep fry until golden brown.
5. When it's done, transfer the chicken onto a plate lined with paper towels. Continue with a new batch to deep fry. Serve immediately with slices of lemon.

Recipe Notes

Quick Tip: Make sure to deep fry only a few pieces at a time so the oil temperature will not drop too low. If the oil temperature is too high, Shio Koji can be easily burn before the chicken is cooked through. If you are not sure if the chicken is done, use a knife to cut the thickest piece of chicken and check inside.

Homemade Koji Rice

Koji rice (and koji barley) is used to make miso, sake, amasake, rice vinegar, soy sauce and mirin. Learn how to make homemade koji rice by growing koji kin mold on rice or barley.

Prep Time: 15 minutes | Cook Time: 15 minutes

Yield: 4 cups | Method: Fermented

Ingredients

- 2 cups rice (white, or polished brown)
- 1/4 tsp koji-kin culture

Instructions

1. Rinse your rice until the water runs clear (to remove all the starch).
2. Soak your rice in water for 8-12 hours.
3. Steam (not boil) the rice until it's softened, but still sticky (see notes for advice).
4. Cool the rice to room temperature.
5. Thoroughly mix the culture into the rice.

6. Spread it out in a baking dish (to maintain the right amount of moisture). Cover with a damp cloth and maintain at 90 F (30 C) for 48 hours.
7. Stir every 12 hours to break up the clumps and evenly distribute moisture. It is finished after 48 hours, when white mold fibers start to develop. (Don't let it go longer than that or it will spore).
8. Store in the freezer until you are ready to use it.
9. See below for incubation options and to learn how to save your own koji-kin mold spores for future batches.

Notes

- Since this is a longer ferment it's important to keep everything clean.
- You can also used pearled barley, and follow the same procedure to make barely koji.
- For steaming, I recommend using a vegetable steamer or colander lined with a tea towel. Just boil the tea towel in the steamer to sanitize it before using it to steam your rice.

Made in the USA
Coppell, TX
05 July 2024

34279220R00066